Answers to Skeptics' Questions

Evidence for the Resurrection

- **Was Jesus a Real Person?**
- **Is There Any Evidence That He Rose from the Dead?**
- **Can We Trust the Witnesses?**
- **Could There be Another Explanation?**

ROSE PUBLISHING

Skeptics' Objections

What is the Resurrection?

The Bible teaches that Jesus is the Son of God, and that he was crucified and died for the forgiveness of sin, was resurrected from the dead, and lives today.

Around AD 30, Jesus of Nazareth was crucified during the reign of Roman Emperor Tiberius (AD 14-37), in the province of Judea. After dying on the cross, he was buried in the tomb of a prominent Jewish leader named Joseph of Arimathea.

Early on Sunday after his crucifixion, several women who had followed Jesus, including Mary Magdalene, Joanna, Mary the mother of James, and Salome, went to Jesus' tomb intending to anoint the body with spices and ointments. The women wondered who would roll away the stone for them. Suddenly, there was an earthquake and an angel appeared. The women found the tomb empty. They feared something had happened to the body of Jesus. An angel of the Lord assured the women that Jesus was alive and had risen from the dead.

Leaving the tomb, the women went to tell Jesus' disciples what had happened. Before they reached the disciples, Jesus himself appeared to the women. Over the next few weeks Jesus appeared to more than five hundred others proving that he had risen from the dead, and verifying all that he had claimed.

Over the centuries, skeptics have developed several objections to the resurrection of Jesus and have proposed several alternative theories about what actually happened to the body of Jesus Christ. Many believe that Jesus' resurrection is too difficult to prove beyond a reasonable doubt. Here is evidence to answer those doubts.

Skeptics' Objections

OBJECTION 1: JESUS WAS A MYTHOLOGICAL FIGURE

Did Jesus of Nazareth even exist? If he did exist, what proof is there that he was crucified?

ANSWER: **Evidence for Jesus Christ comes from many written documents from the first century.**

- 39 ancient sources (in addition to the New Testament), such as Pliny, Josephus, and the Talmud, refer to the life of Christ, his teachings, crucifixion, and/or resurrection.

- Ignatius was a church leader, pupil of the apostle John, and lived only 70 years after the crucifixion of Jesus. Before he was martyred for his faith, Ignatius wrote the following concerning Jesus, "He was condemned: He was crucified in reality, and not in appearance, not in imagination, not in deceit. He really died, and was buried, and rose from the dead."[1]

- An early creed or statement of faith found in the Bible was probably written from 8 to 20 years after the death of Jesus. The creed states that Jesus "was buried, and that he rose again the third day according to the scriptures." (1 Corinthians 15:3-8) Most critical historians agree that documents take more than 20 years to become corrupted by mythological development.

- Several witnesses report appearances of Christ after the resurrection. These reports are recorded in the Gospels, the apostle Paul's letters, and other letters in the New Testament. These accounts were dated from 25 to 60 years after the death of Jesus. If Jesus did not exist, or if the information within these documents were false or corrupt, those who knew Jesus, either friend or enemy, would have objected to the misinformation.

- Peter wrote that the disciples did not follow invented stories when they told people about the power of Jesus, but that they were eyewitnesses to Jesus and his majesty. (2 Peter 1:16)

Closing Statements

ON PENTECOST, 50 DAYS AFTER THE RESURRECTION OF JESUS, PETER ADDRESSED THE CROWD AND SPECIFICALLY POINTED OUT:

- **Everyone there knew that Jesus of Nazareth was a man accredited by God by miracles, wonders, and signs. (Acts 2:22)**
- **Everyone there knew that Jesus was crucified, and that his death was by God's set purpose and foreknowledge. (Acts 2:23)**
- **Everyone there knew that David spoke about the resurrection of Jesus in the Psalms nearly 1000 years before. (Acts 2:24-31)**
- **Everyone there was a witness to the fact that Jesus was raised to life. (Acts 2:32)**

Upon weighing the evidence, it overwhelmingly supports that Jesus Christ is Risen. He is Risen Indeed!

References

1. Roberts, Alexander and James Donaldson, editors. *Epistle of Ignatius to the Trallians, Early Church Fathers Ante-Nicene Fathers to A.D. 325*, Vol. 1.
2. Lewis, C.S., *Mere Christianity*, New York, NY: Macmillan-Collier, 1960. pp. 55-56.
3. Peter W. Stoner, *Science Speaks* Chicago: Moody Press, 1969, 109.
4. Strobel, Lee, *The Case for Christ*, Grand Rapids, MI: Zondervan, 1998.
5. Josephus, *The Antiquities* 20.200.
6. Montgomery, John W., *History and Christianity*, Downers Grove, Ill.: InterVarsity Press, 1971.
7. Geisler, Norman and Thomas Howe, *When Critics Ask*, Wheaton, Ill.: Victor, 1992.
8. Ramsay, W. M. *The Bearing of Recent Discovery on the Trustworthiness of the New Testament*, Grand Rapids: Baker Book House, 1953.
9. Dr. Gary Collins cited in Lee Strobel, *The Case for Christ*, Grand Rapids, MI: Zondervan, 1998.
10. McDowell, Josh D. *The New Evidence That Demands a Verdict*, Nashville, TN: Thomas Nelson, 1999.
11. Corsinii, Raymond J. *Encyclopedia of Psychology*, Vol 2, New York, NY: John Wiley and Sons, Inc.. 2001.
12. Strobel, Lee, *The Case for Easter*, Grand Rapids, MI: Zondervan, 1998, 2003.

Skeptics' Theories

Theory 3: Jesus' Body Was Stolen

The Gospel of Matthew as well as writings of early writers, such as Justin Martyr and Tertullian, suggest that Jesus' opponents explained the empty tomb with a widely circulated story that Jesus' disciples came by night and stole Jesus' body while the guards were asleep. (Matthew 28:13-15)

This is not true because:

• Matthew's Gospel says this cover-up theory was a lie. Matthew reports that the soldiers were bribed by the Jewish priests and elders in order to keep the truth a secret. They were told what to say. How could the soldiers know the disciples stole the body of Jesus if they were all sleeping?

• The enemies of Jesus took several steps to prevent the disciples from stealing the body, such as sealing the stone and providing a guard of soldiers to watch the tomb.

• The soldiers at the tomb would not sleep for fear of death. When they witnessed the empty tomb, they informed the Jewish leaders about what they had seen.

• During the crucifixion, the disciples were cowards who had abandoned Jesus. One disciple denied that he knew Jesus (to a young servant girl). The disciples did not understand his purposes, nor the importance of the resurrection. These men did not have the courage to pass by the guard at the tomb, silently move the extremely large stone, rob the grave, and leave undetected.

Theory 4: Everyone Went to the Wrong Tomb

Every person who witnessed the empty tomb was peering into the wrong tomb. Jesus' body was in a different location.

This is not true because:

• The women observed where Jesus' body was laid only a few days earlier.

• After hearing the report from the women, Peter and John ran to the tomb without directions from the women. It is unlikely that Peter and John would make the same mistake as the women.

• If Jesus' body were still in its correct tomb, his enemies could have produced the body immediately.

• Even if everyone went to the wrong tomb, Joseph of Arimathea, the owner of the tomb, would have corrected them.

Skeptics' Objections

OBJECTION 2: JESUS WAS JUST A MAN

Even if Jesus did exist, he wasn't everything his followers claimed he was. If anything, he was a compassionate person and a charismatic leader. He was a great prophet and teacher, but he was not God.

ANSWER: **Evidence supports that Jesus was all he claimed to be.**

Jesus claimed to be the Messiah (John 4:16-26) who came from heaven. (John 8:21-30) Jesus also claimed to be eternal (John 8:52-59), equal to God (John 10:24-39), and the savior of the world who would die for the forgiveness of sin and would rise from the dead on the third day. (Matthew 26:26-32)

Jesus performed many miracles and signs that supported his claims. Jesus performed miracles of healing (Matthew 8:2-4; Mark 7:31-37), miracles of nature (John 2:1-11; Matthew 8:23-27), and miracles of restoring life. (Matthew 9:18-26; John 11:1-44) The miracles of Jesus were performed in public and could not be contested by Jesus' enemies. On the day of Pentecost, Peter said that Jesus proved his power and authority by performing miracles, wonders, and signs. (Acts 2:22)

Jesus is either what he claimed, a madman, or worse. Knowing the things that Jesus claimed and did, most people would agree he was a moral and upright teacher. In addition, biblical scholars suggest that one cannot say "Jesus was a great teacher, but not God." C.S. Lewis writes in *Mere Christianity*, "I am trying here to prevent anyone saying the really foolish thing that people often say about Him [Jesus]: 'I'm ready to accept Jesus as a great moral teacher, but I don't accept His claim to be God.' That is the one thing we must not say. A man who said the sort of things Jesus said would not be a great moral teacher. He would either be a lunatic—on a level with the man who says he is a poached egg—or else he would be the Devil of Hell. You must make your choice. Either this man was, and is, the Son of God, or else a madman or something worse."[2]

Jesus fulfilled many ancient prophecies. More than one hundred prophecies found in the Old Testament were fulfilled in Jesus Christ. Statistician Peter Stoner[3] reports that the probability of just eight of these prophecies about one person being fulfilled by chance is 1 in 100,000,000,000,000,000. Consider the chances of one person from the line of King David, being born in Bethlehem, entering Jerusalem on a donkey, being betrayed for 30 pieces of silver, crucified, buried in a rich man's tomb, and rising from the dead. Out of all the prophecies fulfilled in Jesus, more than fifty were fulfilled by his death and resurrection.

Jesus predicted he would suffer, die, and rise again. Months before his crucifixion, Jesus told his disciples that he [Jesus] must suffer many things and be rejected by the elders, chief priests and teachers, and that he must be killed and after three days rise again. (Mark 8:31)

Skeptics' Objections

Objection 3: Jesus' Followers Made It All Up

After Jesus died, his followers invented a plan to deceive the entire world into believing that Jesus was the promised Messiah, the fulfillment of Scripture, and the Son of God who rose from the dead.

Answer: **Evidence suggests that such a deception is highly unlikely.**

People will not knowingly die for a lie. The disciples were not fearless liars who wanted to fool the world. After the crucifixion, the disciples fled in fear for their lives. However, once they saw, touched, and spoke with the risen Lord, their lives were transformed. Filled with the Holy Spirit, the disciples left their former jobs and entered a life of telling about Jesus, and as a result endured hunger, persecution, abandonment, imprisonment, suffering, torture, and death. Former journalist Lee Strobel writes, "People will die for their religious beliefs if they sincerely believe they're true, but people won't die for their religious beliefs if they know their beliefs are false."[4]

Furthermore, all of Jesus' followers doubted the resurrection until Jesus physically appeared to them; then they believed.

- The women at the empty tomb were afraid and thought someone had stolen the body. Once Jesus appeared, the women worshiped him and shared the news with the disciples. (Matthew 28:1-10)

- The disciples did not believe the women's report of the empty tomb. They did not believe until Jesus appeared before them.

- Thomas did not trust the testimony of the other disciples. He requested to see and touch Jesus in order to believe. Once he did see Jesus, he believed.

- James, the brother of Jesus, was embarrassed when Jesus preached in Nazareth. (Matthew 13:55-56) He may have doubted the resurrection. However, after encountering the risen Lord (1 Corinthians 15:7), James became the leader of the Jerusalem church and, according to Josephus, was stoned to death because of his faith.[5]

- Saul of Tarsus was a Pharisee and strongly opposed Christians (followers of Christ). Saul opposed this new movement so much that he persecuted believers and assisted in the execution of early Christians. When the risen Christ appeared to Saul on the Damascus road, Saul was completely transformed. Saul, also known as Paul, became one of the greatest followers of Jesus. Throughout his lifetime, Paul was continuously persecuted and imprisoned for preaching the good news of Jesus. Paul's letters to churches and pastors eventually made up 13 books of the New Testament.

Skeptics' Theories

Theory 2: Jesus Did Not Die on the Cross

The Roman soldiers nailed Jesus to the cross, but he did not die there. Rather, Jesus passed out, was removed from the cross, and was placed in the tomb. Later, Jesus was revived and left the tomb in a weakened condition.

If this were true, then:

- Jesus had to survive massive blood loss, torture, and a stab wound in his side.

- The Roman soldiers, who were well acquainted with crucifixion, would have failed in their duties. Furthermore, if the soldiers failed, they would have received the death penalty.

- The Roman soldiers broke the legs of the two criminals crucified next to Jesus in order to speed up their death. If Jesus were still alive, they would have done the same to him.

- Witnesses saw that when Jesus was stabbed in the side, water mixed with blood poured out, medically indicating that Jesus had already died.

- No one questioned whether Jesus was dead or alive while they prepared his body and completely wrapped it in linen.

- Every eyewitness of his death would have been mistaken.

- While suffering from the wounds on his back, in his side, and in his feet and hands, Jesus had to roll the stone away (which normally would take several men to accomplish), sneak past four or more soldiers, and then walk several miles on the road to Emmaus.

- According to studies of first century tombs, the tomb was likely sealed by a 2000-pound rolling stone that fit in a sloping track, which would have been impossible for a sole individual to move from the inside of the tomb.

- There would likely be a record or a witness to Jesus dying at a later time.

Dr. Alexander Metherell, a medical doctor and research scientist, comments on this theory saying, "After suffering that horrible abuse, with all the catastrophic blood loss and trauma, he would have looked so pitiful that the disciples would never have hailed him as a victorious conqueror of death; they would have felt sorry for him and tried to nurse him back to health."[12]

Skeptics' Theories

THEORY 1: THE EYEWITNESSES HALLUCINATED

All of the appearances of a living Jesus after his death were mere hallucinations.

THIS IS NOT TRUE, BECAUSE:

- More than 500 people could not have the same hallucination. Psychologist Gary Collins writes, "Hallucinations are individual occurrences. By their very nature only one person can see a given hallucination at a time."[9]

- Those who saw Jesus after his death did not expect to see him and were surprised by his being there. Psychiatrists agree that hallucinations require expectation.[10] A psychiatric study performed in 1975 suggests that the content of the hallucination "reflects the efforts [of the one experiencing the hallucination] to master anxiety to fulfill various wishes and needs."[11]

Skeptics' Objections

OBJECTION 4: THE WITNESSES WERE UNRELIABLE

There were no impartial witnesses who could verify the physical resurrection of Jesus Christ.

ANSWER: **The reliability for the resurrection is supported by many witnesses, and by the lack of evidence from the opposition.**

Anyone wishing to make up a story in the first century would not use women as their primary witnesses. All four gospels agree that the first eyewitnesses to the proof of Jesus' resurrection were women. On the surface, this does not seem like a major proof for the resurrection. Some may argue that these women, who were very close to Jesus, are not objective witnesses.

The significance of these eyewitnesses lies in understanding the role of women in first century Judea. During the time of Jesus, a woman's testimony was considered worthless. In fact, a woman was not allowed to serve as a witness in court. If early believers wanted to fabricate the resurrection, they would have come up with witnesses who were men who had political and religious influence in their community. Instead, the writers reported the actual witnesses who were women and also close friends of Jesus. Those who recorded these events wanted to be accurate.

No one ever produced the body of Jesus. John Warwick Montgomery says, "In 56 AD Paul wrote that over 500 people had seen the risen Jesus and that most of them were still alive (1 Corinthians 15:6). It passes the bounds of credibility that the early Christians could have manufactured such a tale and then preached it among those who might easily have refuted it simply by producing the body of Jesus."[6] The greatest weapon against these early eyewitnesses would have been to produce the body of Jesus. That weapon was never used, because it didn't exist. The silence of those who opposed Christianity while Jesus' followers preached about the empty tomb only confirmed the fact that the tomb really was empty and its vacancy could not be explained otherwise.

Skeptics' Objections

Objection 5: The Physical Resurrection of Jesus was Not That Important to the Early Church

Christianity began as a moral and philosophical movement. The resurrection of Jesus was a later mythological theory rather than an early historical reality.

Answer: **Sociological evidence suggests that the resurrection was a historical event.**

The drastic social change in faithful Jews is evidence of the resurrection. For thousands of years, Jews endured persecution, oppression, and were scattered over the face of the earth. Unlike every culture around them, the Jewish people never lost their cultural and religious identity. Only a few years after the crucifixion, more than 10,000 Jews embraced the teachings of Jesus Christ and his followers. These early Jewish Christians continued to worship on the Sabbath, but they began worshipping on Sundays as well to mark the resurrection of Christ. As the church matured, they continued to worship on Sundays and referred to those days as "Little Easters." One reasonable explanation for the transformation of so many Jews is that they, or people they knew, had seen Jesus Christ after he rose from the dead.

Early church practices celebrated the resurrection. Jesus' followers were baptized when they first believed and then they would gather together to celebrate the Lord's Supper.

- Baptism celebrates the resurrection. (Romans 6:4; Colossians 2:12) By going under water, the believer remembers the death of Jesus, and by being brought out of the water, the believer identifies with Jesus rising to new life.

- In the Lord's Supper, believers eat bread and drink wine as a memorial to the suffering and death of Christ, as Jesus requested before he died. The Scriptures suggest that the Lord's Supper is a time of joy. (Luke 24:30-35; Hebrews 12:2) There is joy because believers recognize that with the crucifixion there is death, but with the resurrection there is eternal life.

These two practices would not have been carried out if the resurrection had not been a central component to the Christian faith.

Skeptics' Objections

Objection 6: The New Testament is Not Reliable

The New Testament is not historical and the information found in it is unreliable. The Bible has been translated too many times to trust its authenticity.

Answer: Archaeology and history supports the Bible's reliability.

Luke, the physician who wrote the Gospel of Luke, was proved to be an accurate historian. Theologian Norman L. Geisler examined Luke's references to 32 countries, 54 cities, and 9 islands, finding not one single mistake.[7] Renowned archaeologist and historian Sir William Ramsay writes, "Luke's historical accuracy, supported by archaeological evidence, provides credibility to his depiction of Jesus Christ and the accuracy of his writings. Luke is a historian of the first rank; not merely are his statements of fact trustworthy, this author should be placed along with the very greatest of historians. The book of Luke is unsurpassed in respect of its trustworthiness."[8] If Luke was so particular about the minor details, he most likely would be just as particular about the important ones.

The Bible we have today is remarkably true to the original writings. Of the thousands of copies made by hand before AD 1500, more than 5,300 Greek manuscripts from the New Testament alone still exist today. The text of the Bible is better preserved than the writings of Plato and Aristotle. In addition, the discovery of the Dead Sea Scrolls confirmed the reliability of the Old Testament.

Objection 7: The Resurrection is Not Important

Why should it matter whether Jesus Christ rose from the dead?

Answer: If it is true, there are eternal consequences.

The physical resurrection of Jesus Christ is important only if it is true. If Jesus did not rise from the grave, then the unbeliever is no worse or better off than before. However, if Jesus did rise from the dead, then it is reasonable to believe that everything Jesus claimed is true. If what Jesus claimed is true, then he died for the sins of the world and one receives eternal life by believing in Jesus.

The apostle Paul told skeptics in Athens that God wants all people everywhere to repent because he has set a day when he will judge the world by Jesus. He has given proof of this by raising him from the dead. (Acts 17:16-33) Paul asserts that Christ has indeed been raised from the dead. (1 Corinthians 15:20-22)

ROSE PUBLISHING

Published by Rose Publishing
an imprint of Tyndale House Ministries

www.hendricksonrose.com

RELIGION/ Christian Theology/ Apologetics

ISBN 978-1-89094-797-2

9 781890 947972

Printed in the United States of America. 210322SCG

474X *Evidence for the Resurrection*